Soccer Strategies

A FIREFLY BOOK

Published by Firefly Books Ltd. 2009

First printing

Publisher Cataloging-in-Publication Data (U.S.)

Fairclough, Paul.
　　Soccer strategies : attacking, defending, goalkeeping / Paul Fairclough.
[104] p. : col. photos. ; cm.
Summary: A concise guide intended instruct and enhance soccer skills, including attacking, defending and goaltending.
ISBN-13: 978-1-55407-519-5　(pbk.)
ISBN-10: 1-55407-519-X　(pbk.)
1. Soccer.　I. Title.
796.334/2 dc22　　GV943.F357 2009

Library and Archives Canada Cataloguing in Publication

Fairclough, Paul
　　Soccer strategies : attacking, defending, goalkeeping / Paul Fairclough.
ISBN-13: 978-1-55407-519-5
ISBN-10: 1-55407-519-X
　　1. Soccer—Training.　I. Title.
GV943.F34 2009　　796.334　　C2009-902284-2

Published in the United States by
Firefly Books (U.S.) Inc.
P.O. Box 1338, Ellicott Station
Buffalo, New York 14205

Published in Canada by
Firefly Books Ltd.
66 Leek Crescent
Richmond Hill, Ontario L4B 1H1

Printed in China

Soccer Strategies

ATTACKING
DEFENDING
GOALTENDING

PAUL FAIRCLOUGH

FIREFLY BOOKS

Attacking

Contents

He shoots, he scores! Thierry Henry strikes with power and accuracy to find the net for France.

INTRODUCTION

Sheer joy: putting the ball in the net is what attackers are all about.

THEY CALL IT THE GLORY GAME

The famous Brazilian, Pele, once called soccer "the Glory Game." Arguably the greatest player of all time, Pele played more than 1,000 senior games and scored more than 1,000 goals. He won three World Cups — the first when he was just 17 — and gained worldwide fame that lasted long after he actually retired from playing soccer.

His sheer joy for the game — especially scoring goals — was obvious in pictures from his playing days. And you only have to look at any newspaper or soccer magazine to see players celebrating scoring.

Perfect poise: Spain's Raul about to shoot for goa

Goals — and glory — are what the game is all about. It is not always the attackers, or forwards, who score the goals, but it is their job on the field to do so, or to lay on chances for their teammates. Some of the best attackers manage to score goals despite close marking from defenders. Other attackers are more cunning. Spain's Raul scores his fair share of goals, but also often makes clever runs to confuse defenders and help his colleagues to score.

This book will help you develop many of the tricks of the attacker's trade, such as shooting and being in the right place at the right time. It will show you how to lose your marker and how to be a real team player by giving your pals a chance to score.

Above all, it will try to show how improving your skills can be fun — and help you get even more enjoyment out of "the Glory Game."

PROFILE OF AN **ATTACKER**

Soccer is all about goals. Some players seem to have a talent for scoring them, like electric-paced Englishman Michael Owen, dynamic Dutchman Ruud van Nistelrooy and brilliant Brazilian Ronaldo. But were they born with a gift for goal scoring — or have they learned how to do it?

Much is down to natural talent. But one thing is for sure — all these players practice very hard every day. I have seen Ronaldo in training. He's an amazing athlete with a sharp soccer brain. But the thing he has in common with Michael, Ruud, and every top attacker, is his huge desire to score.

More importantly, he is not afraid to miss.

Watch any top attacker: he is always on the prowl, looking for even the glimmer of a scoring chance. He is looking for the opportunity to get in front of a defender and get the touch on the ball that will send it into the back of the net. He might see the goaltender fingertip one of his best efforts round a post. But he won't stand there and curse his luck.

Be quick: Michael Owen has the pace to worry defenders.

WHAT MAKES A GOOD ATTACKER?

- Confidence
- Good concentration
- Courage
- Quick reactions
- Strength, athleticism
- Speed off the mark
- Awareness

8

Head down, blast away: a free-kick on its way to the target.

DID YOU KNOW?

Bobby Charlton scored more international goals than any other English attacker. He bagged 49 in 106 games and was a key member of the team that won the World Cup in 1966, along with his brother, Jack. Bobby was knighted in 1994 for his services to soccer.

Best foot forward: being able to use your left as well as right foot will make you doubly dangerous.

A top attacker will keep trying until the final whistle — and may strike it lucky as the defenders tire towards the end of the game.

Remember, it only takes a second to score a goal ... if you want to be a successful attacker, you will have to stay mentally awake the entire game — thinking all the time.

SHOOTING FOR **GOAL**

H ere are some drills you can try with a friend or two to sharpen your shooting skills.

PRACTICE NO.1

Mark out a goal six paces wide. You need one ball and two players — one in goal, one shooting. If there are more of you, take turns as shooter and goalie. Have five shots each, then change goalies.

• Do not kick the ball when it has stopped moving — pass it to one side, then shoot.

GO FOR IT!

Imagine someone is taking a photo of you. Make a good shape with your body (see page 11).

Practice No. 1.

• Try shooting with your left and then your right foot, and try to vary the angle.

Common fault ...

Too many players look up at the goal a split-second before they make contact with the ball, and this stops them hitting the ball in the right place.

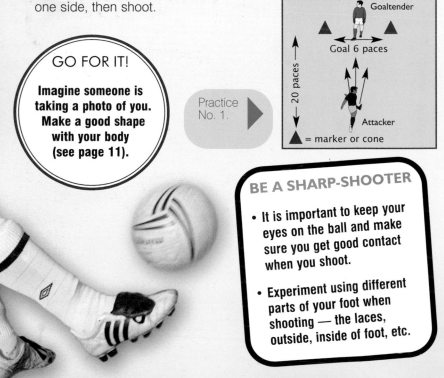

Goaltender

Goal 6 paces

20 paces

Attacker

▲ = marker or cone

BE A SHARP-SHOOTER

• It is important to keep your eyes on the ball and make sure you get good contact when you shoot.

• Experiment using different parts of your foot when shooting — the laces, outside, inside of foot, etc.

PRACTICE NO. 2

Set up a goal as before. Place two markers as shown in the diagram, 20 paces apart, 20 paces from the goal. Cones make good markers.

- The goatender starts with the ball and rolls it towards any spot between the markers.
- As soon as the goalie has let go of the ball, the attacker meets it, and kickes it the first time.
- Have five tries, then change roles.
- Play three sets of five and see who wins the most sets.

BE THE BEST

Try tricking the goaltender. When running to your right, can you kick with the outside of your left foot when he thinks you will use your right? Surprise is a handy weapon to have.

Key point: keep your head down, eyes on the ball.

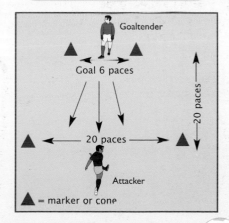

Goaltender

Goal 6 paces

20 paces

20 paces

Attacker

▲ = marker or cone

HEADING FOR **GOAL**

Great attackers score almost as many goals with their head as their feet. It is all about timing and courage! Almost all great attackers master how to head the ball with power and precision. The further from goal you are, the more power you need to get the ball past a goaltender. However, if the cross has been driven hard towards you, a light glance of the head will send the ball on its way into the net.

PRACTICE NO. 1

Make two goals six paces wide, and four apart.

- Serve each other the ball. Try to head the ball past your partner.
- Have ten tries each.
- Once you've mastered this, increase the distance between the goals — the same width, but eight paces apart.

Common mistake ...

Many players let the ball hit them on the head, rather than them hitting the ball with their head.

GO FOR IT!

Keep your eyes open and on the ball — even at the point where your head meets it.

BE THE BEST

Use your forehead when you are heading the ball. Bring your shoulders and neck back, and snap them forward to make contact.

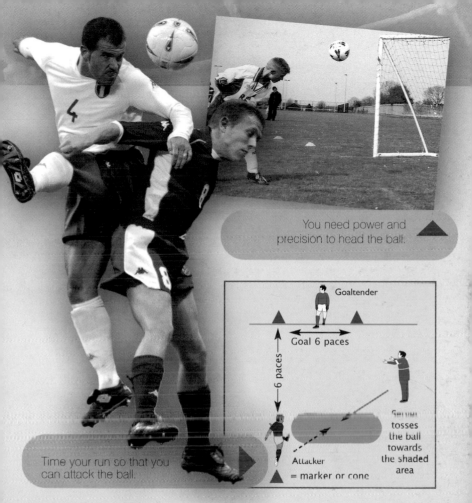

You need power and precision to head the ball.

Goaltender

Goal 6 paces

6 paces

Server tosses the ball towards the shaded area

Attacker

= marker or cone

Time your run so that you can attack the ball.

PRACTICE NO. 2

You need three people for this drill. Set up a goal as shown in the diagram. One player stands 10 paces to the side of the goal, ready to "serve" the ball.

• The server tosses the ball into an area around six paces in front of the goal.

• The attacker stands back a little way and runs forward to head the ball. The goaltender cannot come off his or her line.

• Have five tries from the right, then swap positions. Have five more tries each from the left. Keep score to find the winner.

• The server must provide good crosses — the attacker does not have to accept a poor serve.

Heads up: watch the path of the cross closely, then attack the ball.

BE THE BEST

Try heading into the bottom corner of the goal, on the side where the cross came from.

- The crosser controls the ball, and crosses with his foot to an area just in front of the goal.

- After passing, the attacker makes his run to attack the ball with his head.

- The goaltender is not allowed to come off his or her line, but must remain between the posts.

PRACTICE NO. 3

Once again, you will need three players. Set up the goal and place an attacker 20 paces from the side of the goal.

Have five tries from the right and then swap positions. Have five more tries from the left. Who scores the most goals?

- The attacker passes the ball wide to a crosser.

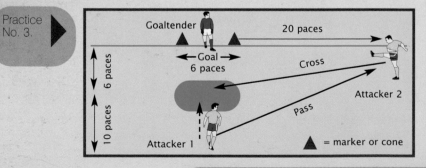

Practice No. 3.

Goaltender   20 paces

←Goal→
6 paces   Cross

6 paces

Attacker 2

10 paces   Pass

Attacker 1   ▲ = marker or cone

Sometimes you have to be brave to take on the goatender as well as the defenders to get in a header.

RECEIVING THE **BALL**

There are some players who always appear to be relaxed when they have the ball at their feet. Players like Ryan Giggs, Steven Gerrard and Aaron Lennon have what coaches call a great first touch.

It doesn't matter how fast the ball comes at these players, or the angle or height of the ball — they have instant control. That gives them more time to do something special with the ball.

You can develop a good first touch — with a little bit of effort.

First, try a very simple exercise you can do on your own, against a wall, but you can also do it with the help of a pal.

Chest the ball down when it comes to you at an awkward height.

Perfect poise: Cristiano Ronaldo kills the ball with precision. See how he uses his arms for balance.

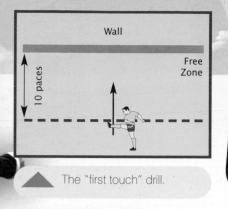

Wall

Free Zone

10 paces

The "first touch" drill.

PRACTICE NO. 1

Stand one pace from an imaginary line, 10 paces from the wall.

- Strike the ball hard, so that it rebounds across the line, then control it.

- If the ball comes away from you, into the area called the 'free zone', keep trying until it doesn't.

- To make it more difficult, you can strike the ball harder and higher.

PRACTICE NO. 2

You need three players for this. Set up a goal, six paces wide, defended by a goalie. A defender should stand with a ball a couple of paces outside the goal post.

- The defender passes the ball to the attacker, who is 15 paces from goal.

- On the attacker's first touch, both the goalie and defender can try to "shut down," or block, the attacker.

No luck this time as the defender clears — but keep trying!

Passes that give you the chance to score have to be clever in order to trick the best defenders. Passes must be quick — and disguised. Great players look one way then pass the other way, because good defenders can work out what is going to happen from watching an attacker's eyes. Defenders don't like the ball being passed quickly into space behind them. It means they have to turn and chase back. Try this with a pal.

PRACTICE NO. 1

Set up two small goals, as in the diagram. Pass the ball to your pal using the goals as a guide. Line up opposite each other, with a goal between you.

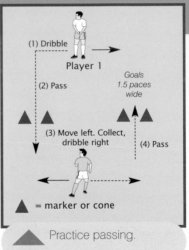

(1) Dribble

Player 1

Goals
1.5 paces
wide

(2) Pass

(3) Move left. Collect, dribble right

(4) Pass

▲ = marker or cone

Practice passing.

• Player 1 dribbles the ball, right to left, until opposite the second small goal (1). Player 2 "shadows" him. Player 1 tries to score through the second goal with a pass to Player 2 (2), then returns to the start.

• Player 2 receives the ball, takes it across to the other goal (3), and tries to score (4).

• Progress: Player 1 collects the ball. Repeat. First to score ten goals wins. Repeat from left to right.

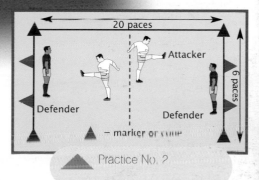

PRACTICE NO. 2

Two attackers take on two defenders for two minutes. Mark out a field using cones. Each defender has to protect one of the goals, and must stay inside their half of the field.

- The attackers work as a team to run the ball through either goal to score. After scoring in one goal, they must then attack the other.

- Each defender can score a point by winning the ball and passing it across the half-way line to his partner.

- The game is restarted when a goal is scored. The ball is given to the attackers in one half, ready to attack the other. After two minutes, swap positions.

20 paces

Attacker

6 paces

Defender

Defender

– marker or cone

Practice No. 2

- Try to make the defender believe you will pass — then dribble past them. Also try to make the defender believe you will dribble — then pass.

GO FOR IT!
If you pass to your friend, carry on running for a return pass.

19

LOSING YOUR **MARKER**

Top attackers make space for themselves by working hard even when they don't have the ball. In 90 minutes, an attacker like Dimitar Berbatov of Spurs might have the ball for just one minute. What he does "off the ball" can have a big effect. He can keep defenders marking him, leaving one of his fellow attackers free, or trick defenders that he is about to run one way — then go another.

GO FOR IT!

Make a pretend or "dummy" movement to create some space for yourself.

PRACTICE NO. 1

Three attackers take on one defender.

• Only one attacker can be on the field, along with the lone defender. The other attackers can move along the sidelines, and call for a pass, but they cannot go on the field.

• The attacker on the field must score a goal after passing to one of the other attackers and collecting the return pass.

• A goal is wiped out each time the defender intercepts the ball. When he does so, the ball is given back and play restarts. Each game lasts for two minutes, then change positions.

• The attackers must all work hard to be ready to collect a pass. The attacker on the field can run in any direction to fool the defender.

Berbatov: more than just the scorer of great goals.

20 paces

Attacker

10 paces

Attacker

Defender

Pass

Attacker

▲ = marker

Practice No. 1.

Outnumbered: it's three against one.

PRACTICE NO. 2

Use the same playing area as before.

- Play two attackers against two defenders for three minutes.

- Rest for two minutes, then play again. Have three games in total.

- To score, an attacker must run with the ball into the goal. Kicking the ball over the line will not count.

BE THE BEST

- Attack (run into) the space behind the defender, even if you do not have the ball.
- If you get free from your marker, you will be ready to receive a pass.
- If the defender gets too close to you, stop your run and come away from him.

GO FOR IT!

Point with your finger to show your teammate where to pass to you. Keep your signals hidden from the defenders.

RUNNING WITH THE **BALL**

The best attackers keep the ball close to them. They don't look down at the ball often when it is at their feet — they know where it is, which means they can keep looking up to see what is going on all around them.

They are aware of their teammates and any space behind the defence. With a burst of speed they can pass their marker — then either fire at goal, or pass to a better-placed pal. Control, awareness and pace make good attackers. Don't just belt the ball past a player and chase it — remember, you need to be in control.

Plenty of fun to be had playing cop and robber.

GO FOR IT!

The robber should trick the cop by suddenly changing direction.

change direction — but the robber must get away from the cop, and the cop must tag the robber.

PRACTICE NO. 1

Two players practice in a field six paces square. One is the "cop" and the other the "robber."

- Each player runs around the area, as fast as possible.

- You can run either way and

- Neither player is allowed inside the square.

- Play for two minutes, then change roles. How often are you tagged? Have two tries each.

- After each "tag," restart on opposite sides of the square.

- Try it once without a ball, then each have one turn with it. Keep the ball under control at all times.

Strong-arm: Ryan Giggs, of Manchester United and Wales, gets away despite being held back.

Try to keep an eye on what the other player is doing, rather than simply watching the ball all the time.

PRACTICE NO. 2

This is a drill for two players. Use the same field as before — just four markers, as shown in the photograph above.

- This is a version of cop and robber — only each player has a ball. This will test your ability to control the ball.
- The idea once again is to "tag" the other player with your hand.

But you also have to keep the ball under control. You cannot tag a player without having the ball under control.

BE THE BEST

Dribble towards the other player, keeping the ball close, but also keep looking up to see where the other player is.

CROSSING THE **BALL**

It's amazing, but true. Almost two-thirds of all goals scored come from crosses. David Beckham is not only a free-kick specialist, but also "assists" with many goals. He has a wonderful ability to deliver the ball from wide or deep positions into the danger area in front of goal for his teammates to score.

The pace and height of the cross are important. Anything over-hit could be straight into the goaltender's arms. Anything under-hit may be easy for a defender to clear.

Crossing from and into the areas shown — to the near or far post — gives your team the best chance of scoring.

Goaltenders do not like the ball being played into these areas, especially if it is traveling quickly.

Best area to cross from.

Best areas to cross to.

GT

Best area to cross from.

Aaron Lennon is a picture of concentration and balance as he prepares to cross the ball.

Hit the target: if your shot finds the net, you will have put in a good near-post cross.

GO FOR IT!

Keep your eyes fixed on the ball as you drive it across.

PRACTICE NO.1

Set up two goals, as shown in the diagram, one as normal, the other to be used as a target for your crosses. Put down a few more markers (like the jackets in the photograph) as a guide for your crossing.

You need a normal goaltender and an attacker waiting for the cross. Another goalie guards the goal that stands between the crosser and the attacker. If you hit this target with your cross, you know you are putting the ball in the near-post "danger zone."

- The crosser dribbles past the marker and then — without the ball stopping — tries to score in the nearest goal.

- Have five tries, then change places with the player guarding that goal.

- Now move this goal and try crossing from the other wing. See who scores most goals.

- This will give you an idea of the type of delivery for a near-post cross — it is driven in, just like a shot.

BE THE BEST

Try curling the ball away from the goal-line, and away from where the goaltender would normally be.

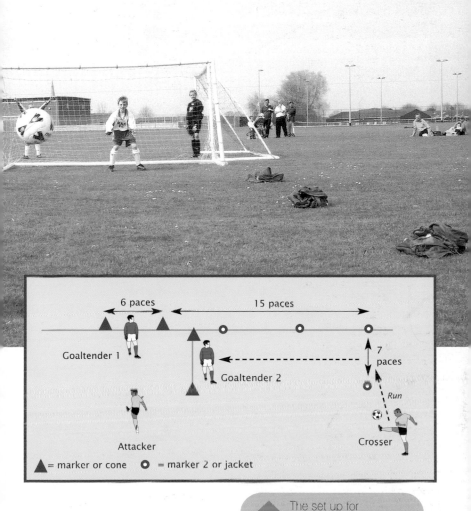

6 paces • 15 paces

Goaltender 1

Goaltender 2

7 paces

Run

Attacker

Crosser

▲ = marker or cone   ○ = marker 2 or jacket

Far-post crosses

The set up for crossing practice.

Repeat the practice, but this time move the target goal back to level with the far post (the second goaltender moves back with it). Fire in your cross towards this second, far-post goal.

You gain an extra point if the goalie in the far-post goal catches the ball above head height. This is the sort of delivery you should be trying to achieve.

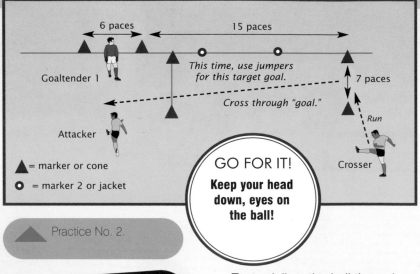

6 paces

15 paces

Goaltender 1

This time, use jumpers for this target goal.

7 paces

Cross through "goal."

Run

Attacker

Crosser

▲ = marker or cone

O = marker 2 or jacket

GO FOR IT!

Keep your head down, eyes on the ball!

Practice No. 2.

PRACTICE NO. 2

Use the same set-up as before, but this time do not use actual posts for the "target" goal — use something flat, like sweaters or coats. This is to make it safe for the attacker, who will be trying to score.

• Try to deliver the ball through the target goal area as before. This time, there is no second goaltender guarding it.

• Try five near-post crosses to the attacker, who tries to score. Then try five far-post crosses.

• The goaltender cannot come off the line.

• Now try five near-post and five far-post crosses from the opposite wing. Each player should have a turn in goal, attacking and crossing.

BE THE BEST

When you cross the ball, don't look up to check out the position of the attacker in the center. Just make sure you deliver the ball into those "killer areas."

TRICKS FOR **ATTACKERS**

Creating and scoring goals is about being clever. Tricking defenders and goaltenders is the key to becoming a successful forward, like Cristiano Ronaldo of Manchester United, the master of the step-over. The element of surprise should never be underestimated, and young players should practice the skills of players like the old Dutch master Johann Cruyff. All the best players have their own set of tricks. Defenders know what they are, but can often do little about them. Now learn some of the tricks of the trade. Better still, can you invent your own trick?

Clever clogs: Ruud van Nistelrooy, left, and Czech star Patrik Berger try the Cruyff turn (see page 30).

The "Cruyff Turn" is named after the brilliant Dutchman Johann Cruyff. It is a great trick to learn to leave defenders completely flat-footed.

Cruyff scored 33 goals in 44 internationals for Holland in a glittering career. Current Dutch star Ruud van Nistelrooy knows what a brilliant trick this is. It makes defenders believe that you are about to strike the ball, but you actually turn back 180 degrees, to the direction that you came from.

▲ Now you see him ... Heading one way, you twist and pull the ball back behind you — leaving the defender on his heels.

PRACTICE NO. 1

Do this on your own, with two markers 12 paces apart.

- Start at one marker and dribble the ball towards the second.

- Shape as if to cross or pass the ball. Instead of striking it, roll your kicking foot over the ball and turn by swivelling on your other foot.

- Use your kicking foot to drag the ball in the new direction (see photograph above).

- Turn your shoulders and hips in the reverse direction to help you to sprint away with the ball in the opposite direction.

BE THE BEST

It takes some getting used to — but the defender won't know where to look! Repeat in the other direction. Attack each marker four times.

Now you don't ... You can see from both pictures that the turn has fooled the defender. The attacker has quickly opened up a growing gap between himself and the opponent.

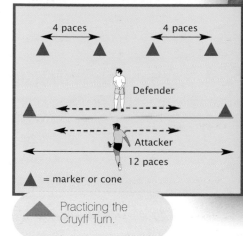

4 paces   4 paces

Defender

Attacker

12 paces

▲ = marker or cone

Practicing the Cruyff Turn.

PRACTICE NO. 2

Set up two small goals, as shown in the diagram above.

GO FOR IT!

Use your arms to make the defender believe you will try to score. This is part of the trick's disguise.

- An attacker, with a ball, stands facing a defender. Start in the middle of the two markers.

- Neither attacker nor defender can cross an imaginary line joining the two markers.

- The attacker approaches either marker. The aim is to pass the ball into one of the goals.

- The attacker can only attempt to score after completing a Cruyff Turn — maximum of four before he must try to score.

- The defender should shadow the attacker to stop him scoring.

- Play six games, three as attacker, and three as defender.

Round the wall: the defenders try to make the block, but the curling shot is on its way into the top corner.

Can you bend it like Beckham? The next attackers' trick is named after former England captain David Beckham, who has the brilliant ability to swerve the ball to deadly effect. It is best practiced with a dead ball — a corner-kick or free-kick. The aim is to be able to make the ball swerve and dip.

BE THE BEST

- The standing foot must be placed slightly behind the ball (normally it would be alongside it).

- To curve the ball from right to left, strike the ball with the inside of your right foot on the lower half, right-hand side. Imagine wrapping your foot around the ball.

- "Cut" across the back of the ball rather than kicking through the center of it. This gets the spin on the ball that makes it bend.

PRACTICE NO. 3

Do this one on your own, or with a pal standing behind the goal to throw the ball back to you to speed things up. Set up a goal and two corner places — each 20 paces from the goal.

- See if you can score without the ball bouncing!

- Have 10 tries from each side: 10 with your right foot and then 10 with your left.

SHIELDING THE **BALL**

One of the key skills for an attacker is to be able to hold on to the ball with his back to goal. This will give his teammates time to get up the field and provide support. If the attacker cannot keep the ball, the attack will break down.

Attackers use their body strength to keep the ball — they spread their arms for balance and to make it hard to force them off the ball. If the defender gets in too close, the attacker can "roll" him (turn away from the defender and get in on goal).

PRACTICE NO. 1

I call this "The Bullfight." Two players are needed. Mark out a square of 10 paces.

- The attacker starts in the middle of the square, with the defender outside the area.

- When the attacker touches the ball, the defender is "live." He must take the ball from the attacker without committing a foul.

- The attacker wins a point if he keeps the ball for 10 seconds.

Keep your body between the ball and the defender.

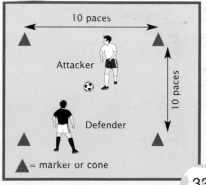

10 paces

Attacker

10 paces

Defender

▲ = marker or cone

PRACTICE NO. 2

Two vs. one. Set up a field 20 paces by 10 paces, with two small goals each four paces wide.

• An attacker starts in one goal with the ball, and the defender starts in the other. The second attacker — the receiver — starts one pace from the defender.

• The game starts when the receiver moves and calls for the ball. The receiver must have more than one touch of the ball. This will help him practice shielding the ball from his opponent.

• Once the ball has been played, both attackers can join forces on the field — two against one.

• Have 10 tries each, and then swap roles. The defender should try to score in the opposition goal. The winner is the receiver whose team scores most goals.

Here is the set up for two vs. one.

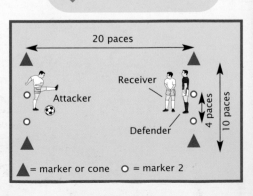

20 paces

Receiver

Attacker

Defender

4 paces

10 paces

▲ = marker or cone   O = marker 2

34

ATTACKER'S **CHALLENGE**

So now you will have learned many of the basics. Remember that practice is now the key if you want to be a good attacker. To wrap it up, try some of the following exercises, to improve your ball control, balance, awareness and speed.

1. Frog's legs

- Your partner stands still, with his legs apart.
- You stand 3 feet (1 meter) in front of him with a ball.
- Pass the ball through your partner's legs.

- Run behind to receive your own pass.
- Pass it back through the legs, then run to collect the ball.
- How many passes can you make in 30 seconds?

2. The chase

- Start on opposite diagonals outside a six-pace square.
- Run two, counterclockwise circuits with the ball.

- You automatically lose the race if you step inside the area.
- Have three separate races.
- Now do the same clockwise.

3. Head to head

- Use a six-pace square, as shown right. An attacker stands in the corner with a ball. The defender stands in the opposite corner.

- The attacker with the ball attempts to "score" by dribbling across either of the red lines. The defender can challenge as soon as the ball is touched.

- Each player has five tries with the ball.

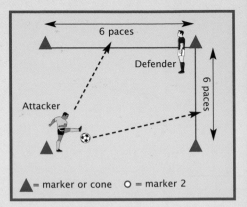

6 paces

Defender

6 paces

Attacker

▲ = marker or cone   O = marker 2

- If the defender wins the ball, he should dribble it across to either line.

4. Head case

- Set up a slalom course using markers that are small and not too high. Set them one pace apart, as in the diagram on the left.

- Dribble through the slalom course.

- When you arrive at the "passing point," pass to the goaltender.

- Then run towards one of the four "gates," and receive a serve from the goaltender. You must head the ball past him into goal. Have four separate attempts, using a different gate each time.

- You have only 15 seconds to score. If this is too easy, agree a reduced time, or add more obstacles.

- Swap over and see who scores most goals.

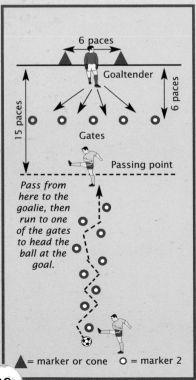

6 paces

Goaltender

15 paces

6 paces

Gates

Passing point

Pass from here to the goalie, then run to one of the gates to head the ball at the goal.

▲ = marker or cone   O = marker 2

Complete player:
Liverpool's
Steven Gerrard.

Defending

Contents

Strong challenge: Tottenham Hotspur defender
Pascal Chimbonda is first to the ball.

INTRODUCTION

Sometimes defenders have to get in where it hurts.

DEFENDERS CAN WIN GAMES, TOO

Winning a game of soccer is all about goals — scoring more than the opposition. But try looking at it another way: you will win if you concede fewer goals than the opposition.

Study any league table in the world, and you will see that the team with the smallest number in its "goals against" column will be at the top of the table or close behind. So a successful soccer team has to have great defenders.

In Italy — a country that has taught the world the value of solid defending — there have been few better central defenders than Fabio Cannavaro or his international teammate Alessandro Nesta. And Paolo Maldini has been an inspiration to a whole generation of Italian youngsters wanting to become full-backs.

Spanish kids have looked up to Fernando Hierro, the French to Lillian Thuram and Marcel Desailly. In the English Premiership, the likes of Rio Ferdinand and John Terry are idols.

But even attackers need to have the basic skills of defending. All good teams "defend from the front."

This means that, when they lose the ball, teams must get players between their own goal and the ball. So, your team's attackers are also your first line of defence.

It doesn't matter where you play on the field, you have to be a good defender, with a grasp of the necessary skills — tackling, marking and passing.

We all marvel at the attacking flair of players like Welsh wing-wizard Ryan Giggs, Italy's Francesco Totti and Frenchman Thierry Henry. We admire the all-round talents of Steven Gerrard and the agility of a host of goaltenders.

But defenders can be just as skilled — and just as important to the end result. The following chapters will show you how.

It's mine! Eyes on the ball, good balance and determination are needed to win the tackle.

PROFILE OF A **DEFENDER**

Defenders come in all shapes and sizes. They are not all giants with thighs like tree-trunks and the flattest of foreheads. Height and bulk helps if you are playing in central defence — and having to mark a bull of a center-attacker like Brazilian superstar Ronaldo or Christian Vieri, of Italy.

Some central attackers are fast. France's Thierry Henry and England's Michael Owen have pace to spare when it comes to taking on defenders. So speed on the turn, speed of thought (anticipation) and positioning, are just as important.

Defenders must be able to head the ball against taller opponents. And they can win it, if their technique and timing is right.

Defenders need a whole range of qualities. The box below gives a list. Some are fairly obvious, and many apply if you are to be successful in any position on the field.

But there are specialist areas, like heading the ball for distance to clear your lines, and tackling without the ball falling free to another attacker.

Keep calm: good control and vision are key assets.

WHAT MAKES A GOOD DEFENDER?

- Calm under pressure
- Confidence
- Courage
- Quick reactions
- Being decisive
- Ability to "read" the game

Getting shirty: Brazil's Roberto Carlos, right, tackles a German forward.

We will look at these areas in greater detail in the following chapters. You will also improve if you watch and learn from better players. Look how much time good players seem to have on the ball — that is no accident. They do it by making sure they are always in the right position, and watching for dangers before they happen.

Defending is sometimes uncomfortable — attackers will be forceful in trying to get to the ball ahead of you.

Courage and strength are key. Defenders don't always get the credit they deserve — just the complaints when the ball ends up in your net!

TACKLING

To win games, a team needs to score goals. But, in order to score a goal, you have to have the ball. You can't score while the other side has it.

The more possession you have, the better your chances of scoring. You can win the ball from the opposition by picking up a pass that goes astray, by being first to a loose clearance or by tackling the player with the ball.

Tackling is an explosive action. But a smart defender will be patient and not dive in. There is nothing more embarrassing than being left on the floor, looking back as an attacker runs on to score!

You need to choose your moment — often when the attacker has knocked the ball a little too far to be in control of it. You will also need to keep him guessing about when you will challenge.

Here are some drills that will set you on the way to becoming a good tackling defender.

PRACTICE NO.1

This is what I call the rope trick. You need two players and a three foot (one meter) long piece of rope, or string. Even a training shirt will do.

- The attacker holds the rope facing the defender, and allows the end of the rope to touch the floor, just in front of the defender.

- The defender pounces forward to try to stamp on, or touch, the rope before the attacker can drag it away. This will test your reflexes!

GO FOR IT!

Any movement of any part of the defender's body will alert the attacker to whip the rope away.

Rope trick: whip the top or piece of string away while your pal tries to step on it.

- Allow the defender to have five attempts, then swap positions.

BE THE BEST

The best posture for a defender is to stand with legs slightly bent at the knees, feet shoulder-width apart. The body should be leaning forward slightly. You should feel balanced and ready to move in any direction.

PRACTICE NO. 2

Let's make things more realistic. Mark out a field as shown in the diagram. Make each goal three paces wide. Use cones if you have them, though sweaters will do. Two of you are needed for this drill.

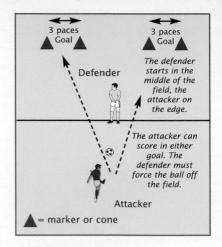

3 paces
Goal

3 paces
Goal

Defender

The defender starts in the middle of the field, the attacker on the edge.

The attacker can score in either goal. The defender must force the ball off the field.

Attacker

= marker or cone

- An attacker starts with a ball on the edge of the field. The defender starts in the middle of the field. The attacker has five attempts to score in either goal.

- The defender must attempt to win the ball and force it off the field.

Pretend to move in one direction, to try to unsettle the attacker.

- After five attempts, change over.

- Keep your scores. Play three rounds in total to see who is the winner.

BE THE BEST

The defender should be patient — don't dive in! Stay on your feet and see if you can work out which way the attacker is going to move. The best time to challenge is when the ball is not fully under control.

HEADING FOR **DEFENDERS**

Generally, when you are in the penalty area and need to clear the ball with your head, you need to get as much distance on the header as you can. All too often weak clearances are picked up around the penalty area and smashed into the back of the net by hungry forwards!

Heading can be difficult, especially when you are being challenged as you try to clear the ball, or a fellow defender gets in your way. It is all about technique and timing.

A good defender can head the ball almost as far as some players can kick it! He will try to kick the ball where one of his own players can pick it up, so that there is no immediate threat of another cross being sent back into his penalty area.

Watch the England defenders John Terry and Rio Ferdinand. When you leap for the ball, and make contact with the head, it is all about timing. The best way to get maximum distance on a header is to use the energy of the ball to send it back in the direction it came from.

Heads up: keep your eyes open when you head the ball clear.

47

PRACTICE NO. 1

For this drill, you will need two players and one ball. Mark out a small field, five paces long, with a goal three paces wide.

- An attacker stands with a ball in the middle of the field. He "serves" the ball with his hands — just toss it up — so the defender can head it back over the attacker's head.

- The defender should try to score in the goal (this is a special goal — the cross bar is as high as the moon!) Height and distance are the aims of this exercise.

- If the defender scores without the ball bouncing, he receives a bonus point.

- The attacker can try to prevent the goal by using his hands, like a goaltender.

- Have five tries each, then swap positions, but don't accept a poor serve that you can't head decently.

BE THE BEST

- **Head through the bottom half of the ball. This will send it high.**
- **Attack the ball — be aggressive. This will give the ball distance.**

Tip: keep your mouth closed to avoid biting your tongue.

Practice: head it back at the server.

FURTHER PRACTICE

Make a field 12 paces long.

- The defender can run from outside the area to head the ball.

- The same rules apply as before.

GO FOR IT!

Try leaping from just one foot. Arch your back and neck, and attack the ball.

BE THE BEST

- Swing your arms in an upward motion to help you gain height. Be careful not to handle the ball.

- As you are in the air, bend your knees and lift your ankles up towards your behind.

Now extend the field to 15 paces.

- The attacker serves the ball, either with a drop-kick from his hands (volley), or from the ground.

- The attacker serves from the goal. Remember, this goal has no crossbar, so you can head it as high as you like.

- Have five tries each and keep score.

49

CONTROLLING THE **BALL**

A defender often has to clear the ball first time in desperate situations. But there are occasions when he or she becomes the first point of attack.

It is then that the defender must be able to bring the ball under control before delivering a precise pass. The best defenders have excellent ball control. No matter what height the ball comes to them, they can master it in a moment. Here is a mental image which will help you to understand more clearly: if you put a blanket over a washing line and then kicked the ball at the blanket, what would happen?

The ball would hit the blanket and drop motionless to the ground.

Why? Because the blanket absorbs all the energy of the ball by "cushioning" it, caving in at the moment of impact and absorbing that impact.

If you want to "kill" the ball, then the part of the body that meets it must behave like the blanket and absorb all the energy of the ball, no matter what height.

GO FOR IT!

**Remember!
Cushion the ball like
a blanket.**

Chest-trap: don't push your chest at the ball. Pull it away at impact so that the ball drops at your feet.

PRACTICE NO. 1

Set up a narrow field with goals three paces wide. You need two players and one ball. Both of you stand in a goal.

- Using an underarm throw, try to score in the other goal. The ball cannot go above head height.

- Each player gains a point by preventing the goal, and controlling the ball before it moves one pace away. You cannot use your arms or hands!

- Have ten throws each.

- The winner is the player who secures the ball the most number of times.

BE THE BEST

Be on your toes, ready to move in line with the flight of the ball.

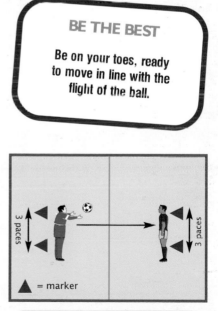

3 paces

3 paces

▲ = marker

Practice No. 1.

PASSING THE **BALL**

If you thought passing was a skill best left to the creative geniuses, think again. It is a skill defenders need, too. You have already found out that the defender can be the first line of attack as he brings the ball out of defence, or if he wins a tackle and finds the ball at his feet.

Pass it right: use the instep to send an accurate long pass, though you can also use the outside of your foot to apply "bend" or spin.

A good, accurate pass is essential if the attack is not to break down straight away. Also, a poor pass straight to an opposing attacker can leave your own defence wide open.

Passing is about keeping possession, and it is very much linked to the subject of the last chapter — control. Once you have comfortably secured the ball, you must then deliver an accurate pass to one of your team.

Defenders should generally pass to their teammates' feet, rather than into space ahead of them. Defenders have the advantage of being able to look ahead to see play develop in front of them, while attackers often receive the ball with their backs to goal.

However, the most important point to stress is that losing possession close to your own goal is a recipe for disaster. That is why the defender must concentrate fully, in order to be accurate with his pass.

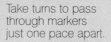

20 paces

Player 2

Take turns to pass through markers just one pace apart.

Player 1

 = marker or cone

PRACTICE NO. 1

Set up a field as shown. You will need two players and one ball for this exercise.

- Each player stands 10 paces from a goal just one pace wide in the middle of the field.

- Each player has 10 attempts to score by passing the ball through the tiny goal.

- Try five passes with the left foot, five with the right foot.

- The goal will be disallowed unless the ball goes through the goal and reaches the other player.

- Have ten tries each. Keep your score: the winner is the player with most goals.

BE THE BEST

When you kick the ball, try to follow through with your foot in the direction of the goal.

Brazilian defender Roberto Carlos shows that good passing is a skill defenders also have to master.

Try using your left foot and your right foot in turns to pass the ball. It will help make you a better player.

PRACTICE NO. 2

Three attackers take on one defender.

- Only one attacker can be on the field, along with the lone defender. The other attackers can move along the sidelines, and call for a pass, but they cannot go on to the field.

- The attacker on the field must score a goal after passing to one of the other attackers and collecting the return pass.

- A goal is wiped out each time the defender intercepts the ball. When he does so, he should give the ball back and play restarts. Each game lasts for two minutes. Then change positions.

- The attackers must all work hard to collect a pass. The attacker on the field can run in any direction to fool the defender.

GO FOR IT!

Try passing the ball into one of the tiny goals with your first touch.

Practice No. 2.

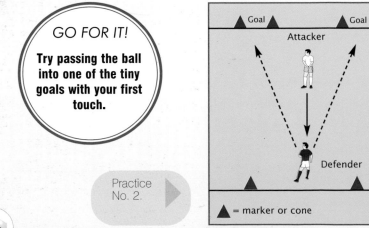

= marker or cone

PRESSING THE **BALL**

When an opponent has the ball, your role as a defender means you must try to prevent him or her from:

- passing the ball forward to a fellow team player
- having a shot at goal
- moving forward with the ball.

The key in each case is to get close to the attacker as quickly as possible, and then assess the situation again. You must not give the attacker room to move, or time to think about his or her options. We call this "closing down the space," or pressing.

The best defenders, like Spain's Fernando Hierro and England full-back Ashley Cole, who is especially quick, close down the space in an instant. Poor defenders complain to their teammates, while an attacker nips between them and the ball rests in the back of their net!

Quick step: get to the player with the ball as quickly as you can, to stop him making the most of the space and time he has to create danger for your team.

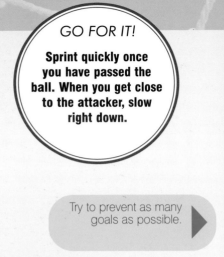

GO FOR IT!

Sprint quickly once you have passed the ball. When you get close to the attacker, slow right down.

Try to prevent as many goals as possible.

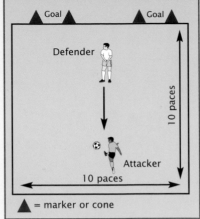

Goal — Goal

Defender

10 paces

Attacker

10 paces

▲ = marker or cone

PRACTICE NO. 1

This drill will get you into the habit of "closing the space down" quickly. Set up a field 10 paces square. Add a couple of goals, as shown in the diagram.

- The defender starts on the line with the ball and passes it firmly to the attacker.

- The attacker must have a minimum of two touches, and a maximum of three, to score in either of the two small goals.

- The defender should sprint forward to prevent the goal attempt.

- Have five attempts each, then try another five. Keep your score. The winner is the defender who prevents most goals.

PRACTICE NO. 2

Use a field 10 paces square with a goal at one end, four paces wide.

- The defender makes a firm pass to the attacker, and must then close the space down quickly.

- This time, make your run slightly curved. The attacker will probably move away from you instead of towards you — a natural response!

- You have started to dictate the attacker's moves and take control. Now try to guide him in one direction.

- Have five tries each, then another set of five. The winner is the one who prevents most goals.

When you get to the attacker, don't dive in to tackle. Let him make a mistake and lose full control of the ball, then make the tackle.

COVERING **TEAMMATES**

Soccer is a team game — but you don't just do things as one 11-player unit. There are at least three mini-teams working together in different areas of the field to make the whole team successful.

Outnumbered: as soon as the attacker gets the ball, he's faced by a defender and one of his teammates.

The backline will work together, talking to, and covering for, each other. So will the midfield and the forwards. If all the mini-teams are working well, then the team as a whole will do well.

There are situations on the field when you need to "back-up" your teammate, who might be struggling to cope with a tough opponent, or may be outnumbered. That is when it is your duty to lend a hand. Assess the situation quickly to see where you need to be in order to help your teammate out best.

If England's Wayne Rooney is about to take on a defender, you can bet that the defender's nearest teammates will be there to offer their support.

DID YOU KNOW?

Former Arsenal defender Tony Adams made his England debut against Spain in 1987, alongside Glenn Hoddle. He later captained the England side managed by Hoddle.

PRACTICE NO. 1

Mark a field 10 paces wide by 20 paces long, with goals four paces wide at either end. Two defenders take on one attacker.

- The defenders line up on the goal-line and one of them kicks the ball firmly to the attacker to start play.

- The attacker should attempt to dribble the ball through the defenders' goal.

- The defenders try to win the ball and dribble it through the attacker's goal.

- Have five tries, then each player changes position. The defenders who score most goals are the winners.

BE THE BEST

One defender should make a fast, curved approach to the ball. Get sideways on to the attacker, "inviting" him to move towards his "trap." The second defender should cover his teammate. It means the first defender can afford to make a tackle, with his teammate ready to steal the ball if it runs loose.

GO FOR IT!

Defenders should be on the "balls of their feet." A quick attacker can race past a defender who is back on his heels.

Waiting game: don't dive in to challenge. Wait for the attacker to lose control of the ball.

Solid tackle: as soon as the attacker looks to have lost control, get in a strong challenge to win the ball.

PRACTICE NO. 2

This drill pits two attackers against two defenders on a field about 30 paces long.

• The defenders start together at one end, and the attackers start together at the other.

• The game starts when the first defender passes the ball to either of the attackers.

• The game is over when the attackers have dribbled the ball over the goal-line, or have lost possession.

• Have five tries, then change roles.

Attackers   Defenders

Pass to
start the
game.

▲ = marker or cone

The defenders must cover each other in this practice.

BE THE BEST

Be patient. If you miss a tackle, make a quick recovery behind your teammate, who is covering you!

STOP AN OPPONENT **TURNING**

When a forward receives the ball with his back to goal, it is important that he is not allowed to turn and attack. As a defender, you have a big advantage. You are already standing between the attacker and your goal, and he is facing the wrong way. But it can all change in a moment. You have to be on your guard.

If players like Didier Drogba or Wayne Rooney are allowed to turn with the ball, they can cause chaos for the opposing team.

It is vital that defenders concentrate at all times, and are ready to close down an attacker to stop him from turning.

DID YOU KNOW?

Fernando Hierro became Spain's all-time top goalscorer, despite being a defender. He played in four World Cups and was an expert at long-range free-kicks. Hierro won European Cup glory with Real Madrid.

Make it tough: don't give the forward (the player in blue) room to turn.

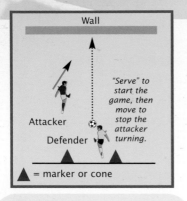

Wall

"Serve" to start the game, then move to stop the attacker turning.

Attacker

Defender

▲ = marker or cone

▲ Move to collect the ball when it comes off the wall, then turn to attack the goal.

BE THE BEST

- Make up the ground quickly, but stop about one pace from the attacker.

- Stoop down low so that you can see the ball from behind the attacker.

- Keep alert and on your toes, and make it difficult for the attacker to turn.

PRACTICE NO. 1

For this practice you will need two players. You can use a wall — or another friend — to be the server.

- The attacker stands 10 paces from the wall. The defender starts with the ball 15 paces from the wall.

- The defender serves the ball by passing it firmly against the wall so that it rebounds to the attacker. The moment the ball hits the wall, both players are "live."

- The attacker has 10 seconds to try to dribble or pass the ball between the two markers.

- Have five tries each, and then repeat twice more. The winner is the defender who prevents most goals.

GO FOR IT!

Don't get too close to the attacker, or he could roll his body against yours and turn.

◄ Be alert: the defender (shown in red) is watching the ball, being ready to tackle or prevent the attacker from passing.

Lean round the attacker to make sure you get a clear sight of the ball.

PRACTICE NO. 2

Set up a field 20 paces long, with a goal at each end six paces wide. This is a two-a-side game. Each team has a defender and an attacker. You will need to mark a half-way line.

- Attackers play in their opponents' half, defenders in their own half. No player may cross the halfway line (see diagram below).

- A defender must remain between the opposing attacker and the goal, unless his own attacker has the ball.

- When his attacker has possession, he can "support" him by getting ahead of the attacker he is marking to receive a pass, but he must stay in his own half.

- As soon as his attacker loses possession, he must ignore the ball and go back to his position behind the opposing attacker.

- The game is over when either team scores, or the ball leaves the field.

- Each team has five tries, then change roles with your teammate, and start again.

BE THE BEST

Be patient: if you force the attacker to pass back to his defender you have done a good job.

GO FOR IT!

Stay alert, but don't expect to win the ball every time.

Attacker must stay in opponents' half.

Attacker 2

Defender 2

Attacker 1

Defender 1

Defender must stay in his own half.

This practice is two-sided.

Team 1

Team 2

▲ = marker or cone

CLEARANCES AND **VOLLEYS**

Playing soccer is about making decisions. Making the wrong decision on the field can have disastrous results! If a defender makes the wrong decision, it can often result in a goal against his team.

Plenty of goals come from defensive errors. Watch a game in your local park or on TV. Think about how a goal was scored. It isn't always down to the individual brilliance of an attacker …

When a defender is under pressure from an attacker he has to clear the ball. Often a defender will try to pass his way out of trouble when a good booted clearance upfield would be a better bet. The best defenders do not take chances!

There is an old saying in soccer: "When in doubt — out!" In other words, if you are unsure what to do, always go for the safest option — the big, booted clearance. In this section, there are two drills designed to give you the feel and confidence of striking the ball.

Good volley: perfect balance, eye on the ball.

PRACTICE NO. 1

You need a big area for this practice — well away from buildings with windows!

- Stand no more than one pace from the goal-line of a goal with a net, or one pace from a washing line with a heavy blanket firmly secured to it.

- Hold the ball in your hands, let it drop to the ground, and kick the ball forward. Have ten tries.

BE THE BEST

- Strike the ball with the laced part of your boot.

- Strike through the bottom half of the ball, not right underneath it.

Power play: volley the ball as hard as you can.

GO FOR IT!

Keep your eyes on the ball as you make contact.

Portsmouth's Matthew Taylor concentrates as he volleys the ball.

PRACTICE NO. 2

Stand one pace away from a goal or blanket, and turn sideways.

- A partner, no more than three paces away, serves you a ball from their hands. The serve should not be above knee-height.

- Volley the ball into the goal or blanket using your right foot. Have five tries.

GO FOR IT!

Your shoulders should be falling backwards slightly as you strike the ball.

- Your partner then serves from the other side, so that you can practice with your left foot.

COUNTERATTACKING

W e have looked at clearing the ball while under pressure from an opponent. But if a defender is not under pressure he can bring the ball under control and start a counterattack.

A defender can also use the counterattack if he breaks up an attack with an interception or tackle. Rio Ferdinand of England and Sami Hyypia, Liverpool's Finnish defender, are very good at setting up counterattacks. Watch games to see how confidently such players bring the ball out of defence. They don't look down at the ball — they look ahead for teammates. Quite often, the other team will back off, giving the defender more time and space than they would give to an opposing forward.

A counterattack should be swift and direct, leaving the opposition players stranded!

PRACTICE NO. 1

Two defenders vs. two attackers. They line up in each half of a small field (see diagram on page 69). The defenders must stay in their half.

• The attackers try to run the ball

across the defenders' goal line — they can't just kick it over, but they can pass to each other.

• The defenders try to win the ball. If they do, they should attack quickly, trying to run the ball into the other goal (don't just boot it).

• If the attackers lose the ball, they must run back to defend their goal.

• When a goal is scored, or the ball goes off the field, the attackers start again with the ball.

• One game lasts three minutes. Then change teams.

BE THE BEST

• The defenders should try hard to anticipate the attackers' passes.
• A defender's pass to his teammate should be quick and accurate.

Defenders

Attackers

*Attack one end first,
then the other.*

▲ = marker or cone

Win the ball,
then bring it out
of defence and
pass it to the
the attacker.

Perfect poise:
look ahead at
how the game is
opening up —
not down at the
ball — when
you start a
counterattack.

GO FOR IT!

It is unsafe to counterattack, then 'clear your lines' — get the ball off the field!

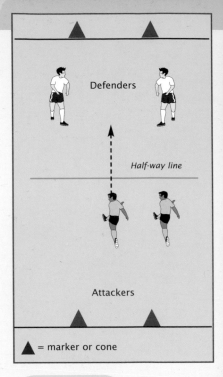

Defenders

Half-way line

Attackers

▲ = marker or cone

▲ Practice No. 2.

PRACTICE NO. 2

This practice is an extension of the last one. Two attackers against two defenders.

- To score, the attackers must dribble the ball across the goal-line — not shoot at the goal.

- If the defenders win the ball, they should try to score in the opposite goal by dribbling the ball across the line as before. But only one defender may cross the half-way line with the ball at any time.

- One defender should make a fast break into the other half, while the one with the ball looks to pass it to him.

- The game lasts for three minutes, then reverse roles.

- Keep score — the team with the best goal-difference will be the winner.

No way past: Jonathan Woodgate of Middlesborough stands firm against Ryan Giggs.

Goaltending

Contents

England's Ben Foster about to launch an attack.

INTRODUCTION

Brilliant Brazilian goaltender Marcos turns the ball around the post.

WANTED: A COOL HEAD

Goaltender is one of the most important positions on the field. He or she is the last line of defence — and often the first line of attack. To be a good goaltender you will need courage, a cool head, quick reflexes — and a loud voice! You will need to "boss" your own defenders, perhaps to tell them when an opposing forward has been left unmarked.
 If you think you can handle it, you're halfway there. Confidence is important. So too is a clear understanding of the job, the rules of the game and the skills you need to be a better player.

You are unique and important. You might not be able to win a game by scoring a goal, but you could still be the game-winning hero by keeping out the other team. You might even make a winning save in a penalty shoot-out.

This section teaches you the basics — how and when to catch or punch the ball, where to position yourself, and how to become the best goaltender you can be.

Diagrams and pictures take you through a series of drills to sharpen your skills with one or more friends — and you will have a lot of fun doing them.

Remember, it takes a lot of hard work and practice to get to the top in anything — and goaltending is no exception!

"It's mine!" American goalie Siri Mullinix keeps a close eye on the ball.

PROFILE OF A **GOALTENDER**

Goaltenders are like well-built cars — they go on for ever. While most outfield players hang up their boots at age 35, top goaltenders can still be at their peak at 40. Often the difference between a good goalie and an outstanding one is experience. The younger you start, the more you can learn, so get that No. 1 jersey on now …

Sometimes group of kids playing a game in their local park will pick teams, only to find no one volunteers to be goalie.

Someone gets thrown the gloves — or the job is shared among teammates, with each taking a turn between the posts.

Every player should try being a goaltender to see if they have a passion or a natural talent for it.

WHAT MAKES A GOOD GOALTENDER?

- Calm under pressure
- Confidence
- Courage
- Quick reactions
- Being decisive
- Being mobile and athletic

Gianluigi Buffon, of Italy, saves a shoot out penalty — every goaltender's dream!

It can be lonely when the action is at the other end of the field, but good goaltenders are always involved. They watch the play move round the field, they are quick to spot any danger — and they make sure they are in the right position to save. Good goalies make the job look easy.

Of course it takes a lot of practice, even if you have natural talent. But you can make all the difference to the result of a game.

After a few saves, you will want to be your team's goalie every week — even if someone else decided you should be in goal in the first place …

THE **STANCE**

Success comes from learning the basics. That's why we start with the stance. Get it right and many of the other skills will fall into place.

This goalie is in the correct stance. Here are the key points to remember:

- Stand on TIP-TOES
- FEET shoulder-width apart
- HANDS at waist height
- BALANCED BODY — your weight should be even on each foot
- KNEES forward, slightly bent
- EYES on the ball.

PRACTICE NO.1

This exercise needs two players. Mark out a goal and field, as shown in the diagram on page 79. Cones are ideal, but sticks, bags, bottles or even jackets will do!

Your friend, the attacker, has the ball and dribbles it slowly from left to right, starting at the first corner marker.

As he moves across the face of the goal, he turns to face the goal every few seconds and threatens to shoot.

The goaltender's task is to "shadow" him by moving across, opposite the attacker. Each time he threatens to shoot, get into the "good stance."

You should get a feel for the "good stance" and be ready whenever you expect a shot.

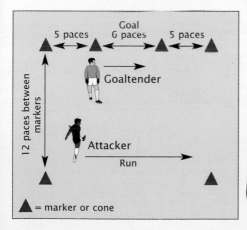

Ready and waiting: the goaltender takes up the ideal stance.

Practicing your stance.

Goal
5 paces | 6 paces | 5 paces

12 paces between markers

Goaltender

Attacker
Run

▲ = marker or cone

BE THE BEST

- The goaltender should not jump sideways. He should "slide" across — almost like a crab — always keeping in contact with the ground so that he can react instantly.
- When the Attacker threatens to shoot, "freeze" in the ready stance.
- Have five tries, then swap positions.

HANDLING THE **BALL**

There are three important rules a goaltender should always follow when handling the ball:

1. Get your body behind the ball whenever possible.
2. Gather the ball to your chest to protect it.
3. Cushion the ball gently — you do not want it falling away from you.

Even under pressure from an attacker, a good goalie will try to get his hands and body right behind the ball.

Kneeling technique: keep your hands and legs behind the ball.

GROUND SHOTS

There are two ways to collect the ball from the ground — either stoop forward or kneel down behind the ball. The position of your head, hands and feet are very important. When you stoop, keep your feet together so the ball doesn't slip between your legs.

	Stoop technique	Kneeling technique
Feet	Close together	Sideways kneel
Hands	Behind the ball, palms out, then cup the ball to chest	Behind the ball, palms out, cup the ball to chest
Head	Steady, eyes follow the ball	Steady, eyes follow the ball

WAIST-HIGH SHOTS

Only the position of the foot changes here. Good habits come as much from what you do with your feet as with your hands.

Feet	Shoulder width, weight equally balanced on either foot
Hands	Palms outwards, cup to waist/chest
Head	Steady, eyes follow the ball

CHEST-HIGH SHOTS

Not a lot of difference here from dealing with the ball at waist height. Relaxing the chest is important — as the ball can bounce away if you stand too rigidly.

Feet	Shoulder width, weight balanced
Hands	Palms outwards, cup ball, relax chest
Head	Steady, eyes follow the ball

BALL ABOVE THE HEAD

Even great goaltenders have been left embarrassed by failing to gather a high ball cleanly.

Sometimes in a game, you will be under pressure from opposing attackers. You may even have your own defenders in your way.

Having a safe pair of hands when the ball is in the air will give your team confidence.

Feet	Shoulder width, weight equally balanced on either foot
Hands	Behind the ball forming a W-shape with the thumbs, relaxed fingers, secure ball into the body
Head	Steady, eyes follow the ball

Germany's Oliver Kahn gathers the high ball in safety.

Spread your fingers behind the ball.

HANDLING PRACTICE

Measure two goals, three paces wide, ten paces apart. Two play, and you will both be goaltenders.

- Throw the ball to each other in turn. The first five times, make sure the ball goes along the ground.

- The next five throws should be below head height — but above the ground.

- Have five more turns, this time tossing the ball above head height.

The next stage:

- Throw the ball to each other, just like the last exercise, again not kicking it.

- Have another 15 throws each, but this time, mix up the order to include five high, five low and five at chest height, so the other player doesn't know what to expect. Remember the good stance and what you should do with your hands and feet.

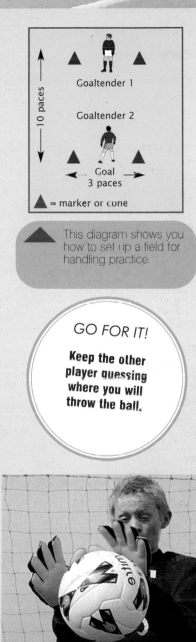

10 paces

▲ Goaltender 1 ▲

Goaltender 2

▲ Goal ▲
3 paces

▲ = marker or cone

▲ This diagram shows you how to set up a field for handling practice.

GO FOR IT!

Keep the other player guessing where you will throw the ball.

NARROWING THE **ANGLE**

You can't make your goal smaller, but you can perform an amazing "magic" trick to make your goal seem smaller to an attacker. If you stay on your goal-line when he approaches you with the ball, he'll have a big space either side of you to shoot at. But, if you come out towards him, you will "narrow the angle." It makes the gaps either side of you appear smaller, giving the attacker less of a target to hit. Coming off your line to narrow the angle also gives you more chance to stop any shot. The attacker will have to hit the ball closer to you to score.

Off your line: suddenly the target has shrunk for the attacker.

PRACTICE NO. 1

You will need some strong string, rope or elastic, about 25 paces long. Tie one end to one goalpost, and the remaining end to the other post (see the diagram below).

- The attacker stands 12 paces away, with the rope round his back, stretched tight.

- As the attacker moves from side to side, he will always be the same distance from goal. When he moves across, so does the goalie.

- The attacker then stops, or "freezes" from time to time. So does the goaltender, who should be able to just about touch the rope with each hand outstretched while in the good stance position.

- Have ten "freezes" each.

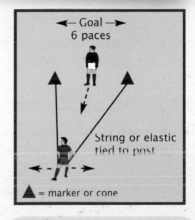

The attacker moves from side to side, and the goalie moves forward to narrow the angle.

BE THE BEST

When you both "freeze," the attacker should allow the goaltender to correct his position so he can just touch the rope with either hand.

GO FOR IT!

Slide your feet as you move from side to side so that you are in contact with the ground at all times.

SHOT **STOPPING**

It is the last minute of an important game and your team is a goal ahead — but under heavy pressure from the other team. You pull off a superb, diving save. You are the hero — even though you did not actually score the winning goal. Moments like that can make all your hard work worthwhile. It is important that, when diving to your side, the hand nearest the ground should be directly behind the ball and your other hand should be slightly on the top of the ball, to prevent it from coming free.

The fans behind the goal think it's in ... but the goalie gets the ball to safety, over the bar.

Safety tip: get your hands behind and slightly on top of the ball like this.

PRACTICE NO. 1

Set up a goal six paces wide. An attacker takes up a position about 15 paces away.

- The goaltender serves the attacker, who must control the ball, move it a couple of paces and shoot.

- Have 10 shots each — the most saves wins!

To make this drill even harder have another friend act as a defender. The defender stands five paces away from the goal post and passes the ball to the attacker. As soon as the ball is halfway to the attacker, the defender can join in and stop the attacker scoring. Have five attempts each.

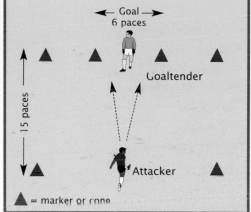

Goal →
6 paces

Goaltender

15 paces

Attacker

▲ = marker or cone

This diagram shows you the drill for shot stopping.

COMING OFF YOUR **LINE**

A goaltender often has to make quick decisions. There is no substitute for experience, but good coaching and practice will help you become a better goaltender. One of the biggest decisions you will have to make is whether you should come off your line. A pass is played between the last defenders and an attacker is clean through with just you to beat! You have to decide: "Do I stay where I am — or go, to try to be first to the ball?" You will have a split-second to make up your mind. If you decide it's "Go!," you must "explode" towards the ball — sprint for it. If you hesitate, chances are you will not get there first.

Be first, be strong — but you have to be quick off the mark, and brave, to steal the ball from the feet of an attacker.

GO FOR IT!

Attack the ball and spread yourself down across the ball. Use a sliding movement.

PRACTICE NO. 1

This drill needs two players. Mark a goal six paces wide and place a ball five paces away.

- You guard the goal. Your pal, goaltender 2, stands still just behind the ball.

- When he gives a signal, you rush out to attack the ball. The signal must not be a spoken command.

- The ball is on the ground, so you will have to slide in.

- Next, place the ball slightly further away and repeat. Get the feeling of "exploding" towards the ball — like a sprinter at the start of a race.

- Have five tries, each time moving further away and from a different angle.

- Now change over and let your pal try. Don't forget, the ball is not moving — you are.

Use this diagram to help you practice coming off your line.

Safety first: gather the ball to your chest and cover it up to stop it running loose.

BE THE BEST

Gather the ball into your body quickly, then stand up. Be ready to throw or kick the ball out.

← Goal →
6 paces

Goaltender 1

5 paces

10 paces

Goaltender 2

▲ = marker or cone

If there are three of you, the third player sits out and gives the "start" command. Then he can take his turn.

- Watch the action closely, even when you are not in goal. You can always learn from others' mistakes or good points. Watching someone else in goal can give you an idea of how you look in that role.

PRACTICE NO. 2

I call this one "Quick on the draw." There's a Wild West feel to it!

- Using the same size goal as before, the attacker and goaltender stand still, five paces from either side of the ball. Wait for a few seconds.

- The goaltender decides to stay back or go for the ball. The attacker tries to score.

- Have five tries each, with the ball at a different angle but at the same distance from goal.

- Swap roles. Each of you try being goaltender five times.

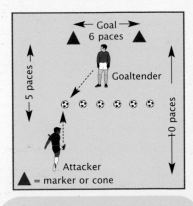

Goal
6 paces

Goaltender

5 paces

10 paces

Attacker

= marker or cone

Here's how to set up your practice for "quick on the draw."

CLEARANCES

Sometimes a goaltender may not have time to catch the ball cleanly, or the ball might be out of reach. At a corner-kick, he might have a crowd of players stopping him getting to the cross. In this case, he may have to punch it clear or deflect it away, to prevent it from being an immediate danger to his goal.

Reach for the stars: goalies have to be strong and decisive to get there ahead of the crowd.

Use the energy of the ball by punching it back in the direction it came from.

GO FOR IT!

The aim is to get the ball as high, wide and as far away from the goal as possible.

The most important thing it is to get the ball away to safety, as far as possible from your goal. Punching clear is important. If you do not get it away by some distance, it might fall in the path of an attacker and you will not be back in position when he shoots. Sometimes, all you can do is to palm or fingertip the ball over your own crossbar or round a post for a corner. This is not ideal — but it is certainly better than conceding a goal!

PRACTICE NO. 1

Set up a goal six paces wide and mark out two more points as in the diagram.

- The attacker tosses the ball in the air, towards the goaltender, from each of the two positions.

- The attacker has five serves from each position.

- When you have mastered this, serve from the other wing.

Toss the ball towards the goalie for him to punch away.

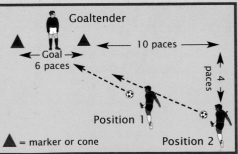

Goaltender
← 10 paces →
← Goal →
6 paces
4 paces
Position 1
▲ = marker or cone
Position 2

92

Keep fists together to make the best contact with the ball.

PRACTICE NO. 2

Now make it more like in a match.

- Repeat Practice No. 1, but this time get a friend to put the goalie under a bit of pressure.
- We don't want the attacker charging in, but he could make a jump to try to head the high ball.

GO FOR IT!

If the ball is catchable, catch it. If it is not, punch it clear. Be decisive.

It is important to get distance when you punch.

BE THE BEST

The extra player is now a distraction to the goaltender. Concentrate hard, and don't be put off by having someone close by going for the same ball. When you get really confident, the server should move the markers slightly further away and can try to kick the ball.

Safety first: If it is not safe to catch the ball, flip it over the bar.

PRACTICE NO. 3

In a game, you often see a goaltender clearing the danger by pushing a cross over his own crossbar. This is because the ball is so close to the goal and, if he doesn't punch the ball properly (it could be wet or muddy), he might end up punching it into his own net!

You will need a junior goal for this one, though the rest of the set-up remains the same. Put markers down either side of the goal.

- Ask the attacker to serve the ball as close to the bar as possible. See if he can make it bounce on the top of the crossbar.

- When you have mastered this, put the goaltender under pressure by using a friend to challenge for the serve. Later, try serving the ball by kicking it, as you would in a real match.

The attacker must serve the ball as close to the crossbar as possible.

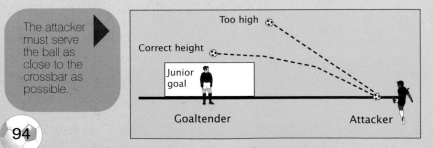

Too high

Correct height

Junior goal

Goaltender

Attacker

GO FOR IT!

The goaltender should have the palm of the hand facing the bar and behind the ball. Push it over the bar with your palm and fingers — don't punch.

You might concede a corner, but a missed punch or catch could give away a goal.

DID YOU KNOW?

Only two goaltenders have captained a World Cup winning side. Giampiero Combi led Italy to their first title in 1934. Dino Zoff skippered the Italians to victory in 1982.

FIRST LINE OF **ATTACK**

When the goaltender makes a save and gathers the ball, he or she becomes an instant attacker. The goalie's speed of thought and the way he "passes" the ball can affect the success of his team's next attack. A goaltender is ideally placed to see the whole field. If the goalie is clever, he will also know the sort of runs and positions his teammates like to take up when he has the ball in his hands, ready to start a quick attack.

▼ "Quick, throw it!" Where would you pass the ball?

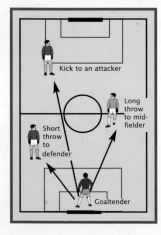

Kick to an attacker

Long throw to mid-fielder

Short throw to defender

Goaltender

Ask yourself these questions ...

❶ Can I put my attackers in with a chance to score? This may mean a long kick behind the other defence.

❷ Can I get the ball safely to an attacker? A long kick will be needed.

❸ Can I get the ball safely to one of my midfield players? This will mean an accurate throw.

❹ Can I get the ball safely to a defender? This means a short, accurate throw.

Rolling the ball out: sometimes your target pass is close — but you still need to take care.

PRACTICE NO. 1

Set up two goals, six paces wide and 15 paces apart.

- Try scoring against your partner by throwing the ball into his or her goal. Have ten throws each, for round 1.

- Have two more rounds, changing ends after each round. The winner is the one who lets in the fewest number of goals!

BE THE BEST

Try out the following throwing actions:

- Overarm, like baseball

- Under-arm, like ten-pin bowling.

GO FOR IT!

Make the save, compose yourself, then throw ...

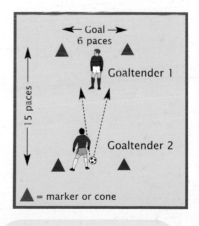

Throw the ball, aiming at the opposite goal.

PRACTICE NO. 2

When throwing the ball to your teammates, make it easy for them to control it. The ball should not go too high.

This practice will encourage a flat delivery of the ball. Remember: the longer your teammate has to wait for the ball, the less time he will have to control it before being tackled.

Make a goal, four paces wide. Mark out two squares either side of it, each two paces wide. Do the same, 15 paces away, as in the diagram.

- Stand in the center of your goal and throw the ball so it bounces in either of the opposing goaltender's squares. You score a point each time you are successful.

- The goaltender will be trying to prevent the ball going in either of his marked boxes.

- Have ten tries each. Who will be the champion?

Aim for the squares on either side of the goaltender.

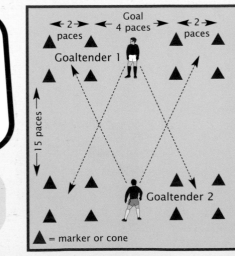

Watch closely: drop kicking the ball means timing your kick just as the ball touches the ground.

GO FOR IT!

Clench your toes the instant you make contact with the ball, for power.

PRACTICE NO. 3

Set up two goals, 25 paces apart. Take turns to try to score. Have five shots using one of the methods below, then five more using the other methods.

- **Volley:** The ball is kicked before it touches the ground after being served from your hands.

- **Drop-volley or half-volley:** You make contact with the ball just as it is it touches the floor having been served from your hands.

- **Ground kick:** The ball is still or rolling on the field.

BE THE BEST

- Keep your eye on the ball at all times.

- Make contact with the center of the ball.

- Strike the ball with your instep (laces).

- Keep your ankle firm.

PRACTICE NO. 4

Set up a goal, six paces wide. Mark four small boxes around a goaltender, 25 paces from your own goal. The second goalie can stand anywhere he likes in the blue zone marked on the diagram.

- Goaltender 2 tries to score against his pal. When goaltender 1 saves, he must try to "score" by throwing the ball in one of the four "box goals." The other goaltender should try to stop him.

- Have five tries each and then change. Repeat twice.

- The winner is the one who scores the most "box goals."

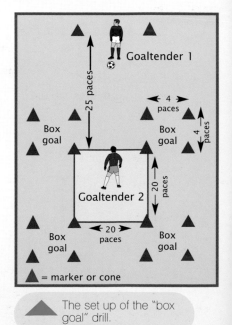

The set up of the "box goal" drill.

THE SKILLS **TEST**

Test all of your new skills in a competition with your friends. The champion is the one who wins most of the nine rounds! In each round you will need to call on many of the key points you have learned.

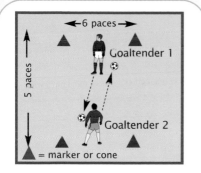

ROUND 1

Measure out the field and goals.

- Take shots at each other.
- The first to make three saves is the winner.

One on one: go through the drills with a friend.

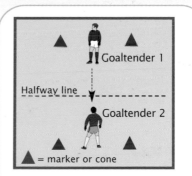

ROUND 2

Use the same field as round 1.

- Goaltender 1 tries to dribble against the opposing goalie, who can only touch the ball once it crosses the halfway line.
- Have four attacks each — the one who makes the most saves, wins.

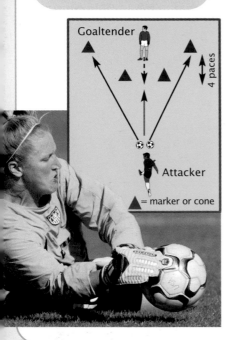

As soon as the attacker moves, the goalie can rush forward.

Goaltender

4 paces

Attacker

▲ = marker or cone

ROUND 3

You need one goal and a smaller goal marked out in front.

- The goaltender stands on the goal-line.

- The attacker has two soccer balls. He must try to shoot through the small goal. With the second ball, he goes for the bigger goal.

- The moment the attacker starts to move, the ball is "live" and the goaltender can rush forward to try to save in the smaller goal.

- The goalie will need to get up quickly to defend his bigger goal from the second shot.

- Have three tries at each goal — big and small — before changing sides. The person with the most saves wins.

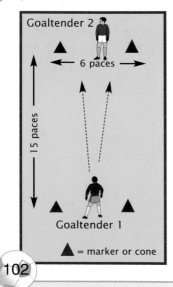

Goaltender 2

← 6 paces →

15 paces

Goaltender 1

▲ = marker or cone

ROUND 4

Play this non-stop for three minutes.

- Each goaltender is allowed only two touches of the ball to score.

- As soon as one goaltender touches the ball, the other can narrow the angle. If a save is made and the ball rebounds into play, the game goes on.

- If a player touches the ball more than twice, a penalty is awarded. The kick is taken 10 paces from goal.

- The winner is the one who lets in the fewest goals.

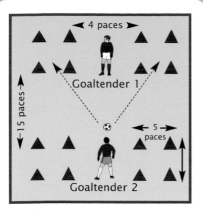

ROUND 5

Set up four squares, each five paces square, as marked.

- One goaltender stands in the space between the squares and tries to throw the ball so it bounces in either of the opposite squares. They are defended by the other goaltender.
- Have four throws each to score in the goal zones.
- The ball must bounce in the zone to count.

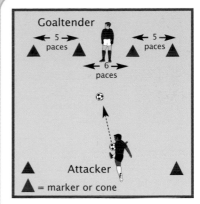

ROUND 7

Mark an area as shown and place two balls as marked.

- The attacker rolls the ball forward and shoots.
- The goaltender tries to save. If the ball rolls outside the zone, or goes wide, both players go for the second ball, which is five paces from goal.
- If the shot with this second ball rebounds off the goalie, the attacker has four seconds to score or the ball is ruled dead.

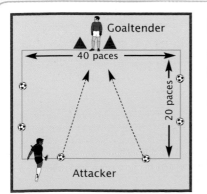

ROUND 6

Set up a goal, six paces wide. Mark an area 40 paces by 20 paces, as shown.

- The attacker will have six shots from different positions around the zone.
- After six, change roles.
- The winner is the goaltender making the most saves.

ROUND 8

Two goalies stand side by side and an attacker is ten paces away.

- As the attacker releases the ball, the two goaltenders try to clear the ball or grab it.
- The goaltenders have three more goes, starting from different stances — kneeling, sitting down and, finally, laying on their stomach.
- The most saves or clearances wins.

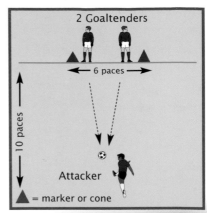

Simply the best: the goaltender with the most saves wins the competition.

ROUND 9

The attacker starts 15 paces from goal with the ball.

- As soon as he dribbles the ball forward, the goaltender can come off his line.
- The attacker has five seconds to score.
- If the attack breaks down — a missed shot or a save — a new attack starts from outside the 15-pace line.
- Swap roles after five tries. The most saves wins.

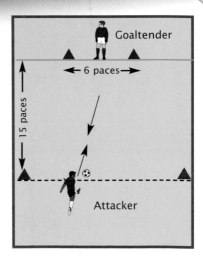